Moments
for
Teachers

Moments
for
Teachers

by
Robert Strand

New Leaf Press

First printing: August 1995
Second printing: March 1996
Third printing: October 1997

ISBN: 0-89221-282-9
Library of Congress: 94-69837

Cover photo and inside photos courtesy of Carroll County Historical Society, Berryville, Arkansas.

All Scripture references are from the New International Version, unless otherwise noted.

Every effort has been made to locate the authors or originators of the stories contained in this book. Most are the result of conversations with pastors, while others were accumulated throughout the course of a 30-year radio and television broadcasting career.

Presented to:

_____

Presented by:

_____

Date:

_____

Miss Thompson

Teddy Stallard certainly qualified as "one of the least" . . . disinterested in school, musty, wrinkled clothes, hair never combed, one of those kids with a deadpan face, unfocused stare. Unattractive, unmotivated, and distant, he was just plain hard to like.

Even though his teacher said she loved all in her class the same, she wasn't completely truthful. She should have known better, she had Teddy's records and she knew more about him than she wanted to. The records showed that while Teddy was a good boy, he had little help from home. His mother was dead, and his father was disinterested.

Christmas came and the boys and girls in Miss Thompson's class brought Christmas presents. Among the presents was one from Teddy Stallard, wrapped in brown paper and Scotch tape. When the teacher opened it, out fell a gaudy rhinestone bracelet with half the stones missing and a bottle of cheap perfume.

The other children began to giggle . . . but Miss Thompson put on the bracelet and some of the perfume on her wrist. Holding up her wrist for the children to smell, she said, "Doesn't it smell lovely?" The children ooohed and aaahed, taking the cue from their teacher.

When school was over that day, Teddy lingered behind. He slowly came over to her desk and said softly, "Miss Thompson . . . Miss

Thompson, you smell just like my mother . . . and her bracelet looks real pretty on you, too."

The next day the children had a new teacher; Miss Thompson had become a different person, no longer just a teacher, but now an agent of God. She truly loved them all . . . but especially the slow ones and particularly Teddy. Soon Teddy showed dramatic improvement!

She didn't hear from Teddy for a long time. Then this note: *Dear Miss Thompson: They just told me I will be graduating first in my class. I wanted you to be the first to know. Love, Teddy Stallard.*

And four years later: *Dear Miss Thompson: As of today, I am Theodore Stallard, M.D. How about that? I wanted you to be the first to know I am getting married next month on the 27th. I want you to come and sit where my mother would sit if she were alive. You are the only family I have now; Dad died last year. Love, Teddy Stallard*

Miss Thompson went to that wedding and she sat where Teddy's mother would have sat!

Today's Quote: *There comes that mysterious meeting in life when someone acknowledges who we are and what we can be, igniting the circuits of our highest potential.* — Rusty Berkus

Today's Verse: Oh, that their hearts would be inclined to fear me and keep all my commands always, so that it might go well with them and their children for ever! (Deut. 5:29).

Kids Go Bald!

In Oceanside, California, in Mr. Alter's fifth grade class, it was almost impossible to tell which boy was undergoing chemotherapy! Nearly all the boys were bald. Thirteen of them had their heads shaved so a sick buddy wouldn't feel out of place.

"If everybody has their head shaved, sometimes people don't know who's who. They don't know who has cancer, and who just shaved their head," said 11-year-old Scott Sebelius, one of the baldies at Lake Elementary School.

For the record, Ian O'Gorman is the sick one.

Doctors removed a malignant tumor from his small intestine, and he started chemotherapy to treat the disease called lymphoma.

Ian decided to get his head shaved before all his hair fell out in clumps. To his surprise, his friends wanted to join him.

"The last thing he would want is to not fit in, to be made fun of, so we just wanted to make him feel better and not left out," said ten-year-old Kyle Hanslik.

Kyle started talking to other boys about the idea, and then one of their parents started a list. Last week they all went to the barber shop together.

The boys' teacher, Jim Alter, also shaved his head.

"You're showing the country and the world what kids can do. People think kids are going downhill. This is the best," Alter said.[1]

To be a compassionate friend is sharing the feelings of sympathy, even sorrow for the hurt and suffering of somebody else. But it goes even beyond these feelings. It has as its reason for compassion the desire to alleviate some of the pain or even to remove its cause. What a wonderful kind of a friend — Ian had 13 of them! Other peers who had enough feeling, humanity, and heart to sacrifice their hair, too. When I am hurting, give me more of that kind of people.

The good Book tells us that in order to have friends, one must be friendly, first. One of the major keys to enjoying a wonderful life is to be a friend and have friends. While you are young is the time to begin establishing those friendships which will last you a lifetime. Who of your friends needs some compassionate understanding in their living?

Today's Quote: *If we don't take care of our friends . . . somebody else will.*

Today's Verse: A man of many companions may come to ruin, but there is a friend who sticks closer than a brother (Prov. 18:24).

The Twenty-six Million Dollar Snub

It was 1884 and a young man and his parents were visiting in Europe. The young man died and his grieving parents returned sorrowfully with his body back home to America.

When the funeral was over the parents began to discuss what might be a fitting memorial to his memory. They eliminated tombstones, ornate graves, or a statue and decided that it should be a living memorial, something that would benefit other young people.

After looking at many possibilities they finally decided that something in the field of education would be most fitting.

An appointment was set to meet with Charles Eliot, then-president of Harvard University. He asked what he could do for them.

Together, they explained about the untimely death of their beloved son and expressed their desire to create or establish a memorial to his memory. Something that would live on to help others like their son to be educated.

Eliot looked at this couple with aristocratic disdain. "Perhaps you have in mind a scholarship," he said crisply and curtly.

"No," said the lady, "we were thinking of something more substantial than that."

Eliot interrupted, "I must explain to you," with a patronizing air, "that what you suggest costs a great deal of money. Buildings are expensive."

There was a pause, the lady got up from her chair slowly and asked, "Mr. Eliot, what has this entire university cost?"

Eliot muttered something about several million dollars.

"Oh, we can do much better than that," replied the lady who seemed to have made up her sharp mind. "Come, dear," she motioned to her husband, "I have an idea." And together they left.

The following year, President Charles Eliot of Harvard heard about the unpretentious couple, who had given $26 MILLION for the memorial to their son.

The memorial was to be built in California and would be named, "Leland Stanford Jr. University."

It can be very costly to mis-judge or pre-judge anyone we meet in life.

Today's Quote: *Who is wise? He that learns from everyone. Who is powerful? He that governs his passions. Who is rich? He that is content. Who is that? Nobody.* — Ben Franklin

Today's Verse: "Do not consider his appearance or his height for I have rejected him. The Lord does not look at the things man looks at. Man looks at the outward appearance, but the Lord looks at the heart" (1 Sam. 16:7).

All I Really Need to Know

ALL I REALLY NEED TO KNOW about how to live and what to do and how to be I learned in kindergarten. Wisdom was not at the top of the graduate-school mountain, but there in the sandpile at Sunday school. These are the things I learned:

Share everything.
Play fair.
Don't hit people.
Put things back where you found them.
Clean up your own mess.
Don't take things that aren't yours.
Say you're sorry when you hurt somebody.
Wash your hands before you eat.
Flush.
Warm cookies and cold milk are good for you.
When you go out into the world, watch out for traffic, hold hands, and stick together.
Live a balanced life . . . learn some and think some and draw and paint and sing and dance and play and work every day some.
Take a nap every afternoon.

Be aware of wonder. Remember the little seed in the styrofoam cup: the roots go down and the plant goes up and nobody really knows how or why, but we are all like that.

Goldfish and hamsters and white mice and even the little seed in the styrofoam cup . . . they all die. So do we.

And then remember the Dick-and-Jane books and the first word you learned . . . the biggest word of all . . . LOOK.

Everything you need to know is in there somewhere. The Golden Rule, love, and basic sanitation. Ecology, politics, equality, and sane living. Think what a better world it would be if the whole world had cookies and milk at 3:00 every afternoon and then laid down with our blankies for a nap. Or if all governments had a basic policy to always put things back where they found them and to clean up their own mess.

And it is still true, no matter how old you are — when you go out into the world, it is best to hold hands and stick together.[2]

Today's Quote: *Arrange to live sensibly, truthfully, and always with a sense of our own limitations.* — Lin Yutang

Today's Verse: Anyone who breaks one of the least of these commandments and teaches others to do the same will be called least in the kingdom of heaven, but whoever practices and teaches these commands will be called great in the kingdom of heaven (Matt. 5:19).

You Never Really Know

• Albert Einstein couldn't talk until he was four years old and couldn't read until he reached seven. He was described by his teacher as "mentally slow, unsociable, and adrift forever in his foolish dreams." He was later expelled from the Zurich Polytechnic School and when he applied for readmittance, was refused.

• When Peter J. Daniel was a fourth grader, Mrs. Phillips, who happened to be his teacher, told him often, "Peter, you're no good, you're a bad apple and you're never going to amount to anything." Peter never did learn to read or write until he was 26. What made a change? A friend stayed with him and read to him the book, *Think and Grow Rich* by Napoleon Hill. Today he owns many of the street corners that he used to fight on and authored his book, "Mrs. Phillips, You Were Wrong!"

• Beethoven was not very good on the violin because he preferred playing his own compositions rather than working to improve his techniques. His teacher said, "You are hopeless as a composer."

• Louis Pasteur was just a very mediocre student in his undergrad studies. Later he ranked 15th out of 22 students in his chemistry major.

• Babe Ruth is considered by many sports authorities and historians to be one of the greatest athletes of all time. Of course he is best known for hitting the most home runs in a season . . . but did you know he also holds the record for most strike-outs?

• Enrico Caruso had parents who wanted him to become an engineer. They were motivated by his voice teacher who said, "He has no voice and could not sing."

• The noted sculptor, Rodin, had a father who said, "I have an idiot for a son." Rodin attempted three different times to gain admittance to an art school. He had been described by a teacher as "the worst pupil in this school." His uncle chimed in by calling him uneducable.

• Fred Astaire took a screen test from the testing director at MGM in 1933. The director wrote a memo: "Can't act! Slightly bald! Can dance a little!" Astaire had that memo framed and hung over the fireplace in his Beverly Hills home.

• Leo Tolstoy, who later wrote *War and Peace*, flunked out of college. They described him as "both unable and unwilling to learn."

Surprise, surprise . . . we just never really know about people. As teachers we must be very careful not to tag, categorize, finalize, or write some people off prematurely. It's easy to be wrong when with some encouragement we might be teaching a future president!

Today's Quote: *Obstacles are those frightful things you see when you take your eyes off your goal.* — Henry Ford

Today's Verse: Jesus looked at them and said, "With man this is impossible, but not with God; all things are possible with God" (Mark 10:27).

Overcoming Obstacles

Life is not always easy! In fact, for most of us life has not been fair and certainly there have been difficulties, trials, and tests. Many of the world's great people have been saddled with disabilities and adversities, but have managed to overcome them. The question is: Were they great people, or did their overcoming the difficulties make them great? Consider. . . .

Cripple him and you have a Sir Walter Scott.

Lock him in a prison cell, take away his freedom, take him out of circulation, and you have a John Bunyan.

Bury him in the snows of Valley Forge, facing an enemy which far outnumbered his troops, and you have a George Washington.

Raise him in abject poverty, make him struggle through political defeat after defeat, let him lose the love of his life, and you have an Abraham Lincoln.

Subject him to a difficult upbringing, expose him to bitter religious prejudice, and you have a Disraeli.

Strike him down with infantile paralysis, take away his legs, and make him dependent utterly on others, and he becomes a Franklin D. Roosevelt.

Have him or her born black into a society which is filled with racial discrimination, and you have a Booker T. Washington, a Harriet Tubman, a Marian Anderson, a George Washington Carver, a Martin Luther King Jr., or a Nelson Mandela.

Make him the first child in an Italian family of 18 children, subject him to abject poverty, gift him musically, and you have an Enrico Caruso.

Have him born of parents who survived a Nazi concentration camp, paralyze him from the waist down when he is four years old, and you have an incomparable concert violinist, Itzhak Perlman.

Call him a slow learner, tab him as being retarded, write him off as being uneducable, and you have an Albert Einstein.

Deafen a musical genius composer and you have made a Ludwig van Beethoven.

Ban him to an island prison, give him visions, and you have a John the Beloved.

Today's Quote: *You can develop an enthusiasm for life. I had a woman who, out of 1,200 salespeople, was the top salesperson in our company. I asked her "How do you do it?" She said, "God didn't make me with an off switch!"* — Danny Cox

Today's Verse: I can do everything through him who gives me strength (Phil. 4:13).

Love and a New York Cabbie

I was in New York the other day and rode with a friend in a taxi. When we got out, my friend said to the driver, "Thank you for the ride. You did a superb job of driving."

The taxi driver was stunned for a second. Then he said, "Are you a wise guy?"

"No, my dear man, I'm not putting you on. I admire the way you keep cool in traffic."

"What was that all about?" I asked.

"I am trying to bring love back to New York," he said. "I believe I have made that taxi driver's day. Suppose he has 20 fares. He's going to be nice to those 20 fares because someone was nice to him. Those fares in turn will be kinder to their employees or shopkeepers or waiters, or even their own families. Eventually the goodwill could spread to at least 1,000 people. Now that isn't bad, is it?"

"But you're depending on that taxi driver to pass your goodwill to others."

"I'm not depending on it," my friend said. "I'm aware that the system isn't foolproof so I might deal with 10 different people today. If out of 10 I can make 3 happy, then eventually I can indirectly influence the attitudes of 3,000 more."

"It sounds good on paper," I admitted, "but I'm not sure it works in practice."

"Nothing is lost if it doesn't. It didn't take any of my time to tell that man he was doing a good job. If it fell on deaf ears, so what? Tomorrow there will be another taxi driver I can try to make happy."

"You're some kind of a nut," I said.

"That shows how cynical you have become. I have made a study of this. The thing that seems to be lacking, is that no one tells people what a good job they're doing."

"But you can't do this all alone!" I protested.

"The most important thing is not to get discouraged. Making people in the city become kind again is not an easy job, but if I can enlist other people in my campaign. . . ."

"You just winked at a very plain-looking woman," I said.

"Yes, I know," he replied. "And if she's a school teacher, her class will be in for a fantastic day.[3]

Today's Quote: *We cannot direct the wind, but we can adjust the sails.*

Today's Verse: Therefore, as God's chosen people, holy and dearly loved, clothe yourselves with compassion, kindness, humility, gentleness and patience (Col. 3:12;NIV).

The Rules for Being Human

1. You will receive a body.

You may like it or hate it, but it will be yours.

2. You will learn lessons.

You are enrolled in a full-time informal school called Life. Each day in this school you will have the opportunity to learn lessons. You may like the lessons or think them irrelevant and stupid.

3. There are no mistakes, only lessons.

Growth is a process of trial and error: Experimentation. The "failed" experiments are as much a part of the process as the experiment that ultimately works.

4. A lesson is repeated until learned.

A lesson will be presented to you in various forms until you have learned it.

When you have learned it, you can then go on to the next lesson.

5. Learning lessons does not end.

There is no part of life that does not contain its lessons. If you are alive there are lessons to be learned.

6. "There" is no better than "here."

When your "there" has become a "here," you will simply obtain another "there" that will again look better than "here."

7. Others are merely mirrors of you.

You cannot love or hate something about another person unless it reflects something you love or hate about yourself.

8. What you make of your life is up to you.

You have all the tools and resources you need. What you do with them is up to you. The choice is yours.

9. Your answers lie inside you.

The answers to life's questions lie inside you. All you need to do is look, listen, trust, and choose rightly.

10. You will forget all this.

11. You will need help with your life.

No one can make it alone in life. All need help. That help is in a relationship with God, Creator of this universe. You choose to invite Him into your life.

12. You can remember it whenever you want.

Today's Quote: *I have a key in my bosom, called PROMISE, that will, I am persuaded, open any lock in Doubting Castle.* — The Pilgrim's Progress

Today's Verse: Keep your heart with all diligence, For out of it spring the issues of life (Prov. 4:23;NKJV).

I Am a Teacher

I am a TEACHER.

I was born the first moment that a question leaped from the mouth of a child.

I am Socrates, exciting the youth of Athens to discover new ideas through the use of questions.

I am Annie Sullivan, tapping out the secrets of the universe into the outstretched hand of Helen Keller.

I am Marva Collins, fighting for every child's right to an education.

I am Mary McCloud Bethune, building a great college for my people, using orange crates for desks.

I am Bel Kaufman, struggling to go "Up the Down Staircase."

The names of those who have practiced my profession ring like a hall of fame for humanity . . . Booker T. Washington, Ralph Waldo Emerson, Leo Buscaglia, and Moses.

I am also those whose names and faces have long been forgotten but whose lessons and character will always be remembered in the accomplishments of their students.

I have wept for joy at the weddings of former students, laughed with glee at the birth of their children, and stood with head bowed in grief and confusion by graves dug too soon for bodies far too young.

Throughout the course of a day I have been called upon to be an actor, friend, nurse and doctor, coach, finder of lost articles, money lender, taxi driver, psychologist, substitute parent, salesman, politician, and a keeper of the faith.

A doctor is allowed to usher life into the world in one magic moment. I am allowed to see that life is reborn each day with new questions, ideas, and friendships.

An architect knows that if he builds with care, his structure may stand for centuries. A teacher knows that if he builds with love and truth, what he builds will last forever.

I am a warrior, daily doing battle against peer pressure, negativity, fear, conformity, prejudice, ignorance, and apathy. But I have great allies: Intelligence, curiosity, individuality, creativity, faith, love, and laughter all rush to my banner with indomitable support.

I AM A TEACHER![4]

Today's Quote: *Once you see a child's self-image begin to improve, you will see significant gains in achievement areas, but even more important, you will see a child who is beginning to enjoy life more.* — Wayne Dyer

Today's Verse: You, then, who teach others, do you not teach yourself? (Rom. 2:21).

Liberal Arts Education

In 1942 the U.S. Navy was desperate for talent. Four young men stood shivering in their shorts while waiting in a small room. A grim-faced selection committee asked the first would-be-officer, "What can you do?"

The recruit replied, "I'm a buyer for Macy's, and I'm trained to judge quickly between markets and prices and trends."

The committee replied, "Can't you do anything practical?" And they shunted him off to one side.

When the committee asked the next man, a lawyer, if he could do anything practical, he said, "I can weigh evidence and organize information." He, too, was rejected.

The third man answered the same question, "I know language and a good deal about history," he replied. The committee groaned in unison and sent him off to the side.

Then the fourth man said boldly, "I'm a college-trained engineer, and I can overhaul diesel engines." The committee wanted to make him an officer on the spot.

By the time the war was over, the Macy's buyer was assistant to the Secretary of the Navy, with many complex responsibilities requiring instant good judgment. He became an expert by taking courses in naval management and government procedures.

The lawyer wound up as assistant to Admiral Halsey, and during a critical battle he deduced from intelligence reports where the enemy fleet was located. He left the military, bedecked with medals.

As for the third man, he got the job of naval secretary to several congressional committees and helped determine the future of American presence in the South Pacific.

And what was the fourth man, the college-trained engineer, doing at the end of the war? He was still overhauling diesel engines.[5]

Interesting how the fates of people can be intertwined about their gifts and talents and education. Who would have thought? This is not a knock against an education. There's a need to keep on learning after we have learned. All of life can be a school, if we will allow the lessons to become part of our personhood. Who knows what might happen in the future? Prepare now, build now, learn now — so that when opportunity comes knocking, you have an answer!

Today's Quote: *It is better to be prepared for an opportunity and not have one than to have an opportunity and not be prepared.* — Whitney Young Jr.

Today's Verse: Do your best to present yourself to God as one approved, a workman who does not need to be ashamed and who correctly handles the word of truth (2 Tim. 2:15).

A Life Preserver

He wasn't the most intelligent, most athletic, or most likely to succeed. Previous teachers warned me he needed extra attention, but they gently agreed he was worth the effort.

Ryan's classmates appreciated his determination . . . from a distance. They were cordial to him but passed knowing looks whenever Ryan said or did something "Ryanish." He ate lunch alone or sat in the library surrounded by books. Occasionally I saw him on the field catching underclassmen's pitches (a totally "uncool" thing for a senior to do).

A struggling first-year teacher, I was feeling alone myself, and as lesson plans tugged at my heels and waves of grading threatened to pull me under, I was drowning in inadequacy.

By late October I had changed my strategy. I would sneak to my room and pray in the serenity of the cool darkness. I would sit in each of my trouble-students' seats and pray for them . . . and for me.

One November day, Ryan tossed me a life preserver. He had asked me that morning for lunchtime help with an essay, but I couldn't find him around campus. Giving up the search, I wandered back to my classroom to ready myself emotionally for the next class.

Approaching my room, I noticed someone inside. The lights were off but a tall figure crouched by my podium. It was Ryan!

He didn't look up when I slipped into the room. He was mumbling with his head bent and eyes closed. I heard my name, a classmate's and a few more . . . that was all, but that was enough. Ryan was praying. I stood beside him and put my hand on his shoulder. He finished and then looked up.

"I've seen you pray for us, Miss Peil. I thought I'd do the same for you," Ryan said with a smile. "I talk to God all the time. He helps me. All the guys feel sorry for me or think I'm weird, but I'm not. They don't realize *they* need God, too."

I've never forgotten Ryan's lesson. In fact, his complete dependence on God has taught me to swim with the current of His love . . . instead of against the flow. When waves of nostalgia ebb over me and I pull out that first year's yearbook, Ryan's picture causes me to smile. Beside his picture he scrawled, "Thanks for helping me understand, Miss Peil. Don't forget me." No Ryan, I owe YOU the thank-you . . . for tossing me a life preserver.[6]

Today's Quote: *Wonderful things happen to all of us when we live expectantly, believe confidently, and pray affirmatively.*

Today's Verse: One day Jesus was praying in a certain place. When he finished, one of his disciples said to Him, "Lord, teach us to pray" (Luke 11:1).

Others and Absent-mindedness

Professors and others of the educated mind have been accused of a notorious human fault — forgetting what, where, when, direction, etc. You possibly remember the old story about the professor who was stopped by a student who had a question. When finished the prof asked which way he had been going before he stopped. The student pointed, "That way, sir." The prof replied, "Good, then I've just had my lunch." Let's hear it for the profs — they may not be the only people of the absent-mind. Read on. . . .

General Yoannes Metaxas, the dictator of Greece from 1936 to 1941, was notoriously absent-minded. Once, while flying as a passenger in a military seaplane he told the pilot that he wanted to fly it for a while. They changed places and after a short flight, Metaxas was preparing to land at the upcoming airport.

"Sir," the pilot said nervously, "this is a seaplane!"

"Of course! Of course!" Metaxas said and turned out over the adjoining bay where he brought the plane down safely. He thanked the pilot, opened the door of the cabin and stepped out into the sea!

Then there is the patient who complained, "What's the matter with me, Doctor? I can't seem to be able to remember anything."

The doctor replied, "Well, when did this problem start?"

Patient: "When did what start?"

Bill Cosby in his book, *Time Flies*, complains about absent-mindedness in this way: "I recently turned 50 . . . and I am having to learn to accept a new me; one who dials a telephone number and, while the phone is ringing, forgets whom he is calling."

The British Royal Navy likes to fondly remember its celebrated vice admiral who died with honors. When his strongbox was opened by the bank, a card inside it met the eyes of the executors of his will: "Starboard . . . RIGHT. Port . . . LEFT."

The noted Captain Frank Winston of Louisa Courthouse, Virginia, had walked the few hundred yards from his house to the railroad depot when he felt his coat pocket and exclaimed, "I do declare, I believe I've left my watch at home! I wonder if I have time to go back and fetch it?" So saying, he took his watch from his trousers pocket and saw it was still 15 minutes to train-time. "Yes, yes," he said, "Plenty of time," and returned back home.

Well, well . . . which way was I headed in this? Oh, well. . . .

Today's Quote: *Don't worry if you start losing your memory. Just forget about it.* — Benjamin Franklin

Today's Verse: Remember your Creator in the days of your youth, before the days of trouble come and the years approach (Eccles. 12:1).

Monsters in the Dark

This story comes from a teacher friend of mine, and highlights in a sobering way the challenges faced by those who stand up every day in front of students.

Arriving late for school one day, "Beth" appeared more withdrawn than usual. Never an outgoing child, she always finished her work on time — quietly, of course — and seemed obsessive about remaining as inconspicuous as possible. Beth was cooperative and pleasant, but the sort of student a teacher can easily overlook in the hustle and bustle of "the daily grind."

But there was something about Beth that was definitely not right this blustery winter day. Maybe it was the subtly vacant expression. Or the mismatched socks — a first for this thoughtful sixth grader.

Breezing through a math lesson, my friend continued to keep an eye on her suddenly intriguing student. As the rest of the class groaned through the study period, my friend concocted a harmless excuse to get Beth outside. Once in the hallway, she asked Beth to tell her what was wrong.

The tears began to splatter immediately, catching the teacher a little offguard. Gathering Beth quickly, she found an empty office where they could be alone, and the story poured out.

Unknown to her mother, Beth's stepfather had been sexually abusing her for some time. Sacrificing herself for her younger sister, this terrified girl had endured a nightmare for more than two years.

That night, Beth stayed with my friend and her husband. My friend phoned home that she had to stay late for a conference, but a sheriff's deputy would be bringing Beth. Upon entering the house, Beth flinched by reflex and asked the husband if he was the only one home.

You see, one fiend had caused Beth to be afraid to ever be alone with a man again. How tragic.

Teachers see and hear our nation's most horrific stories on a daily basis. And they know that there are times when, if our children tell us they are scared of monsters, we must listen.

Then in the darkness, we have the opportunity to tell them about a man who loves them so much He sacrificed himself for us. His name is Jesus.[7]

Today's Quote: *Man's inhumanity to man makes countless thousands mourn.* — Robert Burns

Today's Verse: "Because of the oppression of the weak and the groaning of the needy, I will now arise," says the Lord. "I will protect them from those who malign them" (Ps. 12:5).

Inglisch Spocken Here

The following has been selected and collected for all English teachers who may have made it thus far in this book. These are a collection of notices in what may have been intended to be written in plain English. Upon reading this, our only hope is that somehow our language will survive the Berlitzkrieg. (Berlitz, as in the language school, for the uninitiated.)

From a hotel in Moscow: "If this is your first visit to the USSR, you are welcome to it."

Notice found in a travel agency in Barcelona: "Go away."

A Tokyo hotel has this notice on its elevator doors: "Do Not Open Door Until Door Opens First."

Another Tokyo hotel posted: "Is forbidden to steal towels, please. If you are not person to do such, please not to read notice."

A butcher in Nahariyya, Israel: "I slaughter myself twice daily."

This from a barber in Zanzibar: "Gentlemen's throats cut with nice sharp razors."

Hotel del Paseo, Mexico City: "We sorry to advise you that by a electric desperfect in the generator master of the elevator we have the necessity that don't give service at our distinguishable guests."

This notice was placed on every table in the dining room of a hotel in Columbo, Sri Lanka: "All vegetables in this establishment have been washed in water especially passed by the management."

A dentist in Hong Kong: "Teeth extracted by latest methodists."

Another elevator sign from Tokyo: "Keep your hands away from unnecessary buttons for you."

A hotel in Bucharest posted this notice: "The lift is being fixed for the next four days. During this time you will be unbearable."

Hotel Deutschland, Leipzig: "Do not enter the lift backwards and only when lit up."

From the bakery, Vale of Kashmir: "First-class English loafer."

From a little restaurant in Mexico City: "U.S. Hots Dog."

A barber in Tokyo: "All customers promptly executed."

The Restaurant des Artistes, Montmartre: "We serve five o'clock tea at all hours."

Don't you love this? What a delight! How about a hand for all those marvelous, wonderful people who have composed such signs and sentences! I only hope they never open any English dictionaries as long as they promise to keep on writing such notices.

Today's Quote: *To err is human, but if the eraser wears out before the pencil, you're overdoing it a bit.* — National Motorist

Today's Verse: He who answers before listening — that is his folly and his shame (Prov. 18:13).

Birdcages in the Mind

Most creative people aren't happy unless they are challenged by a problem that needs to be solved. Such people can't look at anything without thinking about how it could be improved, bettered, adapted, modified, or changed for the better, of course.

One such person was Charles F. Kettering, inventor who did so much for the automobile industry, especially General Motors Corporation. He laid the foundation for much of what we see in the car industry today. He loved to compare his kind of thinking, mind exercising, to "hanging birdcages in the mind."

Kettering had a friend and colleague who made a bet with him. If he were given a birdcage and hung it in his house in a prominent place, sooner or later this friend would have to buy a bird for the cage. The friend jumped at the bet.

So Kettering on his next visit to Europe — Switzerland to be exact — purchased this very beautiful and ornate birdcage for his friend. "I got him an attractive birdcage made in Switzerland," recounted Kettering, "and my friend hung it near his dining room table. Of course, you know what happened. People would come in and say, 'Joe, when did your bird die?' 'I never had a bird,' Joe would say. 'Well, what have you got a birdcage for?' people would ask. Finally, my friend Joe said it was simpler to buy a bird than to keep explaining why he had an empty birdcage."

Kettering, who loved to recount this little story, would conclude, with a grin on his face: "If you hang birdcages in your mind, eventually you get something to put into them."

Teachers should be hanging empty birdcages in the minds of all their students! What an opportunity! The next time you're asked, "What do you do for a living?" You can graciously say, with a grin: "My job is to hang empty birdcages in people's minds." You can be sure once again that this will be a great conversation starter. I love it.

A Gallup Poll survey indicated that in the people surveyed, success is equated with good health, jobs they like, and happy families. This same survey also pointed out that the traits most common in successful people are: purpose in life, the willingness to take risks, to be able to exercise control, to solve problems rather than place blame, they care about quality of life, and they have opportunity to share their expertise and knowledge. All life elements that make for excellent teachers and the hanging of birdcages!

Today's Quote: *Don't be afraid of the space between your dreams and reality. If you can dream it, you can make it so.* — Belva Davis

Today's Verse: Until now you have not asked for anything in my name. Ask and you will receive, and your joy will be complete (John 16:24).

This First Grade Teacher Is Blind

Marjorie West was born with sight but has been progressively going blind. "Retinitis pigmentose" attacks the retina and in turn causes night blindness, the loss of depth perception, and the loss of peripheral sight. At age 46 she was declared legally blind.

"The Lord and I have proven the doctors wrong several times," she says. "I was told my retina wouldn't let me teach beyond 50, but here I am still going strong." Marjorie, seven years later, can still see a bit . . . like looking through a soda straw. She still keeps up with more than 20 rambunctious first grade students. All by herself? Not really. If you visited her first grade classroom of the Glennon Heights Elementary School in Colorado you would find Rush, her seeing eye dog, resting under her desk.

You would notice her full-time assistant, Karen Taylor, who has loaned her eyes since 1987 to be the look-out to help maintain order in this classroom. There is really only one more distinctive sign allowing for Marjorie's blindness . . . it's the way in which the kids identify themselves when responding orally.

It's been tough. Back in 1987 when the school board was told by Marjorie about her progressive disability, she was ready to fight for her job at all costs! She, with confidence, made her appeal to be allowed to be a contributor in the Jefferson County district. She even offered to be re-trained, if they deemed it necessary. Also, there were laws which the district had to follow in making some reasonable accomodations for the handicapped, provided her performance was good. Her excellent reputation preceeded her, which was also a help in being retained as a teacher.

Today she is thought of as friendly, an overcomer, nurturing, committed, and professional. Outstanding could also be added to this list, as well as a teacher who has continued to learn.

She sums up her life this way: "The process of going through loss myself . . . not only my eyes, but divorce, giving up driving, my father's death . . . helped me become more sensitive to the needs, the fears, the feelings, and all the things kids bring to school with them." Her physical weakness has become an asset!

Today's Quote: *I pray myself through every day. I need prayer, because just like these kids, I face new fears daily.* — Marjorie West

Today's Verse: But he said to me, "My grace is sufficient for you, for my power is made perfect in weakness." Therefore I will boast all the more gladly about my weaknesses, so that Christ's power may rest on . . . I delight in weaknesses, in insults, in hardships, in persecu-tions, in difficulties. For when I am weak, then I am strong" (2 Cor. 12:9-10).

How to Win Friends and Make Money

Dale Carnegie was what we would call a "late bloomer." He had some early success as a salesman for correspondence courses, then became an outstanding salesman for Packard automobiles, along with a brief stint as an actor. He came to a turning point in his life — he had the vague feeling that all was not right, that there might be more in life for him. So Carnegie began to evaluate himself, to take a look at where he was headed with his life. Among the things he valued was a teacher's certificate, but he didn't know what to teach. What should he do next with his life?

In his evaluation he reached the decision that the most important and valuable thing in his education was that he had learned public speaking. He put together a proposal which he presented to the YMCA and their schools in New York that he should teach courses in public speaking to local businessmen. The YMCA administrators thought so little of the idea that they refused to pay him the $2 per night which he had requested. They would allow him to teach and use their facilities and contact their clientele, but no salary of $2 per night. However, instead, they agreed to give him a percentage of the net profits from these courses. In less than three years, these courses taught by Carnegie became so popular that soon he was receiving $30 and more per night. Word spread. Enthusiasm built a demand for this information. Soon he was besieged with offers to teach public speaking in many other U.S. cities and even in Europe.

Out of these courses came the first of many wildly successful, best-selling books, *How to Win Friends and Influence People, Public Speaking* and *Influencing Men in Business,* and more best sellers. Also as an out-growth, the Dale Carnegie Institute was established which still conducts seminars on a worldwide basis.

There is a story about P.T. Barnum and how he became a victim of his own success. So many people were crowding into his shows that huge lines were forming outside the tents. To facilitate and speed up the turn-around, he placed large signs inside the tent exit which read: "This way to the egress." People, gullible, thinking that "egress" meant another attraction, would eagerly file outside following the show.

So it's my hope that you will find a new adventure outside your tent.

Today's Quote: *Don't try to think why you can't. Think how you can.*

Today's Verse: He who was seated on the throne said, "I am making everything new!" Then he said, "Write this down, for these words are trustworthy and true" (Rev. 21:5).

What Is Vitally Important?

A story is making the rounds about a recently widowed lady who was encouraged by her family to get a parrot to keep her company. "It will be some live creature that can talk to you and help you with your loneliness."

She went to a local pet store where the owner showed her a bird and enthusiastically sold this bird as having a 500-word vocabulary. She returned the next day to the pet store owner to report: "That parrot hasn't said one word yet!" A bit angry I might add.

"Does it have a mirror?" asked the storekeeper. "Parrots like to be able to look at themselves in the mirror. They think it's another bird to talk to."

The next day she was back, even a bit more angry, announcing that the parrot still didn't say a word!

"What about a ladder?" the storekeeper replied. "Parrots enjoy walking up and down a ladder and get so excited that they talk." So she bought the ladder and put it in the cage.

Sure enough, the next day she is back, the parrot will not talk! Not one word! "Does the parrot have a swing? Birds enjoy swinging so much that it induces them to talk." She bought the swing.

Two days later the lady returns to the store, obviously upset, to announce that the parrot had died! "I'm so terribly sorry to hear that, ma'am," said the saddened store keeper. "By the way, did the bird ever say anything, anything at all, before it died?"

"Yes," replied the lady. "It said, 'Don't they sell any bird food down there at that store?'"

Aren't we funny people? We are into readily buying mirrors by which to primp the outward looks; ladders so that we and others can climb higher; swings so that we have the latest and best in entertainment. But where is the sustenance for soul and spirit? And it still holds true that nobody can live on bread alone. Teacher, ma'am, sir, what are you feeding into the minds and spirits of your charges? Think of the implications of molding the life and character and soul and spirit of a human being that will live forever!!

Today's Quote: *I'm amused when other agencies try to hire my people away. They'd have to "hire" the whole environment. For a flower to blossom, you need the right soil as well as the right seed.*

Today's Verse: These are the commands, decrees and laws the Lord your God directed me to teach you to observe in the land that you are crossing the Jordan to possess, so that you, your children and their children after them may fear the Lord your God as long as you live by keeping all his decrees and commands that I give you, and so that you may enjoy long life" (Deut. 6:1-2).

Handicapped?

Tracy MacLeod hates the word "handicapped!" She may use it when she's making jokes about herself to her teammates at Canada's Brandon University, but beyond that, the word does not apply to her. After all, what person with a real handicap would have returned to play basketball only three months after having half of her lower right leg amputated? What person with a real handicap could score 20 points and grab 10 rebounds in 20 minutes of playing time, as the 21-year-old MacLeod did recently against the University of Regina team?

Last season, her first in Brandon, in the southwest corner of Manitoba, MacLeod, a 6'-1" center, was averaging 11.2 points and 6.2 rebounds on two healthy legs.

But that was before one mis-step under the basket launched her into a medical nightmare. While attempting a lay-up in a home game against Winnipeg in January 1993, MacLeod landed awkwardly on her right leg. The crack of her tibia and fibula was so loud that several players covered their ears and turned away.

The leg was set and cast — within 24 hours circulation problems began, necessitating the first of nine operations over the next five months. They weren't successful, and finally the choice was facing a lifetime of corrective surgeries and a misshapen leg which would be useless, or amputation.

In June of 1993 her leg was amputated eight inches below the knee. She went home walking nearly limp-free on a prosthesis 2-1/2 weeks later. No one expected her to show up for the first day of practice in Brandon. MacLeod's doctors told her that a return to her former level of play at any time was an unrealistic expectation.

"I took what the doctors said and just kind of laughed," says MacLeod. "I wasn't about to let anyone put limitations on me. I just wanted to get back to my normal life and basketball was a big part of that life. I didn't know if I could play, but I had to try."

She is a step slower and can't jump as high as before but she moves remarkably well in the paint and still has the best shooting touch on the team. "Her comeback is amazing," says teammate Andrea Brown. "It is a real motivator to see her out there. It makes you think about what you take for granted and how much stronger you could be."

Opponents give her more respect than sympathy. "We play Tracy as tough as we always did," says rival coach, Tom Kendall, of Winnipeg. "If we don't, she scores."

"If they play slack defense, they're going to pay," says MacLeod. "He who hits first, wins. Usually, that's me!"[8]

Today's Quote: *If it is to be, it is up to me!*

Today's Verse: "If you can?" said Jesus. "Everything is possible for him who believes" (Mark 9:23).

The Ultimate Sacrifice

Linda Birtish literally gave herself away. Linda was an outstanding teacher who felt that if she had the time, she would like to create great art and poetry. When she was 28, however, her doctors discovered she had an enormous brain tumor. They told her that her chances of surviving an operation were about 2 percent . . . they chose to wait six months.

She knew she had great artistry in her. So during those six months she wrote and drew feverishly. All of her poetry, except one piece, was published . . . all of her art, except one piece, was shown and sold.

At the end of six months, she had the operation. The night before the operation, in case of her death, she wrote a "will" in which she donated all of her body parts to those in need.

Her operation was fatal. Her eyes went to an eye bank in Bethesda, Maryland, and to a recipient in South Carolina. A young man, age 28, went from darkness to sight. He wrote to the eye bank thanking them for existing. It was only the second "thank you" the eye bank had received after giving out in excess of 30,000 eyes!

Furthermore, he wanted to thank the parents of the donor. He was given the name of the Birtish family and flew to see them on Staten Island. He arrived unannounced. After making his introduction, Mrs. Birtish embraced him. She said, "Young man, if you've got nowhere to go, my husband and I would love for you to spend your weekend with us."

He stayed, and as he was looking around Linda's room, he saw that she'd read Plato. He'd read Plato in Braille. She'd read Hegel. He'd read Hegel in Braille.

The next morning Mrs. Birtish was looking at him and said, "You know, I'm sure I've seen you somewhere before, but I don't know where." All of a sudden she remembered. She ran upstairs and pulled out the last picture Linda had drawn. It was a portrait of her ideal man.

The picture was virtually identical to this young man who had received Linda's eyes.

Then her mother read the last poem Linda had written on her deathbed. It read:

Two hearts passing in the night, falling in love, never able to gain each other's sight.[9]

Today's Quote: *There is a land of the living and a land of the dead and the bridge is love.* — Thornton Wilder

Today's Verse: Once you spoke in a vision, to your faithful people you said: "I have bestowed strength on a warrior; I have exalted a young man from among the people" (Ps. 89:19).

Out of the Pens of Babes

After Christmas vacation, a teacher asked her small pupils to write an account of how they spent their holidays. One youngster wrote about a visit to his grandparents in a life-care community for retired folks:

"We always spend Christmas with Grandma and Grandpa," he said. "They used to live here in a big red house, but Grandpa got retarded and they moved to Florida. They live in a place with a lot of retarded people. They live in tin huts. They ride big three-wheel tricycles. They go to a big building they call a wrecked hall, but it is fixed now. They play games there and do exercises, but they don't do them very good. There is a swimming pool and they go to it and just stand there in the water with their hats on. I guess they don't know how to swim.

"My grandma used to bake cookies and stuff. But I guess she forgot how. Nobody cooks — they all go out to fast food restaurants.

"As you come into the park, there is a doll house with a man sitting in it. He watches all day, so they can't get out without him seeing them. They wear badges with their names on them. I guess they don't know who they are.

"My Grandpa and Grandma worked hard all their lives and earned their retardment. I wish they would move back home but I guess the man in the doll house won't let them out."[10]

Well, I guess, eventually, if we live long enough, this might happen to all of us. And it's refreshing to look at this and other things of life through the eyes of little people. What a different world, delightful. And let's face it, teachers have an opportunity to see a slice of life that few others do — to see and listen and be part of kids up close and personal. What fun to be a part of molding this potential. There is such an innocence and wonder at all of life through the eyes of children. Our challenge is how to maintain this excitement, yet encourage the development of their gifts. It's to direct and not thwart. It's to encourage and not dampen. It's to challenge and not overwhelm. Teaching may be the highest calling of all, because teachers work on eternal lives.

Today's Quote: *Every man must decide whether he will walk in the light of creative altruism or in the darkness of destructive selfishness.* — Martin Luther King

Today's Verse: It would be better for him to be thrown into the sea with a millstone tied around his neck than for him to cause one of these little ones to sin. So watch yourselves (Luke 17:2-3).

He's With Me Now

Storm clouds and strong gusts of wind had come up suddenly over Columbus, Ohio. The Alpine Elementary School radio blared tornado warnings. It was too dangerous to send the children home. Instead, they were taken to the basement, where the children huddled together in fear.

We teachers were worried, too. To help ease tension, the principal suggested a sing-along. But the voices were weak and unenthusiastic. Child after child began to cry — we could not calm them.

Then a teacher whose faith seemed equal to any emergency, whispered to the child closest to her, "Aren't you forgetting something, Kathie? There is a power greater than the storm that will protect us. Just say to yourself, 'God is with me now.' Then pass the words on to the child next to you."

As the verse was whispered from child to child, a sense of peace settled over the group. I could hear the wind outside still blowing with the same ferocity of the moment before, but it didn't seem to matter now. Inside, fear subsided and tears faded away. When the all-clear signal came over the radio sometime later, students and staff returned to their classrooms without their usual jostling and talking.

Through the years I have remembered those calming words. In times of stress and trouble, I have again been able to find release from fear or tension by repeating, "He's with me now."[11]

Life has storms and will continue to have storms. There is no way to escape entirely the storms, tests, and trials of life. It's part of the human condition. There is no way to have any guarantee that life from this moment on will never be filled with storms. But there are plenty of promises that God has given to us from His Word that He will be with us no matter what may come our way. We do everything humanly possible to avoid these storms and attempt to protect our loved ones from their storms, unsuccessfully. The promises are not that we will have a storm-free life, but that in every storm which comes our way, He will be there to comfort, guide, and protect. The promises are for good days and bad days, and every kind in between. He hasn't promised cloud free days, but He has promised strength. Whatever the day or test, He has promised to be there with you. And the bottom line is that there is no positive security in this life but there is a positive promise of strength for each day!

Today's Quote: *They can conquer who believe they can. He has not learned the first lesson of life who does not every day surmount a fear.* — Ralph Waldo Emerson

Today's Verse: For God did not give us a spirit of timidity, but a spirit of power, of love and of self-discipline (2 Tim. 1:7).

The Power of Perseverance

He was born on a Kansas farm and educated in a simple one-room schoolhouse. The country schoolhouse that he and his siblings attended was heated by an old-fashioned, pot-bellied stove, and it was Glenn and his older brother's responsibility to keep the school's fire going in cold weather. This they had to do before the students and teacher arrived so it would be warm for the day.

One morning, Glenn and his brother poured kerosene on some live coals still in the stove and it blew up! Glenn could have escaped but his brother would have been left behind. The brother had been knocked out by the explosion. Instead of escaping, Glenn struggled with the rescue of his brother. Both boys suffered horrible burns. The brother died and Glenn, with severe burns over the lower half of his body, was taken to the nearby hospital. The doctor told his mother that this son would almost surely die, hinting at the fact that it might be for the best. If he should live, this son would likely never walk again.

This brave boy didn't want to die. He determined that he would live, and to the amazement of the attending doctor he survived. But with all the damage to his legs, the doctor reminded his mother again that he would be a lifetime invalid.

Once more this boy made up his mind — he would NOT be a cripple, not be an invalid, he would walk and run! It looked hopeless — the legs dangled uselessly. He was released from the hospital and his mother massaged those legs after the burns had healed. When he was taken outside in his wheelchair he threw himself from the chair on wheels and pulled himself across the grass, dragging those useless legs to the picket fence, where, with great effort, he managed to raise himself to a standing position. He would then walk around the yard, pulling himself along beside the pickets. Soon he wore a path.

With more struggle, daily massages by his mother, an iron will, and determined perseverance he began to stand alone, walk with help, then walk alone. Soon he was running! His goal was to become the fastest human in the mile distance. Soon the sheer joy of running became his life. In college he made the track team and one day in Madison Square Garden, this young man with perseverance ran the mile faster than any human being before him. And who was the burned little boy who refused to give up? Dr. Glenn Cunningham, in his day the fastest human miler!

Today's Quote: *Nothing in this world — talent, genius, and education — can take the place of perseverance.*

Today's Verse: As you know, we consider blessed those who have persevered. You have heard of Job's perseverance and have seen what the Lord finally brought about. The Lord is full of compassion and mercy (James 5:11).

The Cipher in the Snow

It started with tragedy on a cold February morning. I was driving behind the Milford Corners bus, it veered and stopped at the hotel, which was not a regular stop. I was annoyed at the unexpected stop. A boy lurched out of the bus, reeled, stumbled, and collapsed on the snow bank at the curb. His thin, hollow face was white even against the snow. "He's dead," the driver whispered.

It didn't register. I glanced at the scared young faces in the school bus. "A doctor! Quick! I'll phone from the hotel!"

"No use. I tell you, he's dead." The driver looked at the still form. "He never said he felt bad, just tapped me on the shoulder and said, real quiet, 'I'm sorry. I have to get off at the hotel.' That's all."

At school the news went through the halls. "I'd appreciate you going out to tell the parents," the principal told me. "They haven't a phone. I'll cover your classes."

"Why me?" I asked, "Wouldn't it be better if you did?"

"I didn't know the boy, and in last year's sophomore personalities column I noticed you were listed as his favorite teacher."

I drove down the bad road to the Evans' place. His favorite teacher! He hadn't said two words to me in two years!

The ranch kitchen was clean and warm. I blurted out my news somehow. Mrs. Evans reached for a chair, "He never said anything about bein' ailing."

His stepfather snorted, "He ain't said nothin' about anything since I moved in here."

I was to write the obituary for the school paper. "Cliff Evans, never legally adopted by stepfather, five half-brothers and sisters." Meager information and the list of D grades were all. Cliff Evans had silently come in the school door and left in the evenings and that was all. No clubs, teams, nor offices, he had been a nobody, nothing, zero.

How do you make a boy into a zero? The school records showed some of the answer. "Cliff won't talk. Uncooperative. Slow learner," from the third grade teacher. But his third grade IQ was listed at 106 . . . the score didn't drop under 100 until the seventh grade. Even timid children have resilience. It takes time to break them. How many times had he been chosen last? How many had told him, "You're a nothing, Cliff Evans." Then it hit me . . . when there finally was nothing left at all for Cliff Evans, he collapsed on a snow bank and went away.[12]

Today's Quote: *The world seldom notices who the teachers are but civilization depends on what they do and say and are.*

Today's Verse: The King will reply, "I tell you the truth, whatever you did for one of the least of these brothers of mine, you did for me" (Matt. 25:40).

Day 25

One Chance in a Million

Maybe you remember February 20, 1962? If not, I will refresh your memory by telling you that an American astronaut climbed into a space capsule and was hurtled more than a hundred miles into the sky. This capsule went into space orbit and circled the earth three times in the following four hours. Then, with its lone, brave passenger still cocooned in safety, splashed down in the Atlantic Ocean at precisely the spot which had been pre-selected by the crew of people who had sent it aloft.

Millions of people worldwide marveled at such an accomplishment of our scientific thinkers. How is it possible to plan such wonders? Today, it's old hat — we've had men walk on the moon and sent up our re-usable space shuttle many times. How is it possible to predict and plan the exact orbit of our space vehicles?

Much of the credit for such accomplishments has to go to a man whom you nor most Americans have never heard about. This man was born with three strikes against him. John Kepler was born prematurely in the year 1571. He was so tiny and premature at birth that the attending physician gave him only one chance in a million to survive! Somehow he survived!

At the age of four he was stricken with smallpox which left him crippled in both hands and with very weak eyes. Some time later, both of his parents were declared insane and placed in an institution.

He determined to amount to something in spite of the unhappy lot life had dealt him. He would become an astronomer. This is the man who discovered the "three laws of motion" of the planets. He discovered the concept of the convex lenses which make possible the giant telescopes of our day which scan the heavens. That's not all — this man also discovered the foundations upon which the science of calculus is based!

Without John Kepler and his discoveries — laws of planets in motion, the convex lense, and calculus — America's space program would have always remained on the ground! There never would have been a space program. And Kepler, in humility, always acknowledged that God was the source of his life and knowledge and discoveries!

Today's Quote: *It seems to me that if you're bearing pain properly as a leader, whether you're a preacher, a college professor, a parent, or a teacher, you ought to have the marks of the struggle. One ought to have bruised shins and skinned knees.* — Max DePree

Today's Verse: Endure hardship with us like a good soldier of Christ Jesus (2 Tim. 2:3).

This Caring Sensitive Professor

On the first day of class, as had been his custom, this particular college professor asked his Speech 101 students to introduce themselves. And in order to make the names stick with the faces they were to tell what they liked most and least about themselves. The students, in turn, would stand and give their names and what they liked most and least. There were some laughs, a bit of self-consciousness . . . but it was a great class-breaker.

Then . . . the class attention was focused on the next person, a young lady named Dorothy. She did not stand but kept her eyes glued to her desk top. She did not say a word. The professor thought that perhaps she had not heard or was shy and may have needed a bit more encouragement, "Dorothy, Dorothy, it's your turn." Still no response. Then he said it again, "Come on Dorothy. How about you?"

After a rather long pause, she stood but did not turn to face the class. She said, "My name is Dorothy Jackson." Then . . . she spun in the direction of the class and with a sweeping motion of her hand, she pulled her long hair away from her face. There for all to see was a large wine-colored birthmark covering nearly the entire left side of her face. She blurted it out, "Now you *all* know what I like least about myself."

Immediately, this sensitive, caring, professor moved to her side. He gently leaned over her shoulder and gave her a kiss on the birthmark and then followed that with a big hug. He straightened up and said, "That's okay. God and I think you're beautiful."

She began to cry and sobbed for a number of minutes. Other members of this class followed their professor's lead and gathered around her and took turns giving her hugs. After she had managed to gain her composure, she said, "Thank you. I have waited all my life for someone to hug me and say what you said." Dorothy paused, to regain her composure, then quietly, almost in a whisper, "Why couldn't my parents have done that? My mother has never even touched my face."[13]

Don't let anyone tell you that the human touch given in love is not powerful! Incredible! I wish I had the rest of the story to tell you but I would almost wager that Dorothy experienced a break-through. It was a liberating touch. When Jesus Christ came . . . He came to embrace us, to kiss us, even our ugliness, and to show us what the love of the Heavenly Father was all about. And . . . isn't this what we are all about, too?

Today's Quote: *Love is a little four letter word . . . people can make it big.*

Today's Verse: How great is the love the Father has lavished on us, that we should be called children of God! And that is what we are! (1 John 3:1).

It Can Be Done

Life seems to hold at least two kinds of people — negativists and positivists. But we find that the pessimists are more vocal in their expressions of why something cannot be done. It's a whole lot wiser and healthier to listen and become one of those persons who say it can be done! So the next time you are confronted with negatives and negative people, take the time to read again what one very creative, positive thinker has written.

IT COULDN'T BE DONE
Somebody said that it couldn't be done,
But he with a chuckle replied
That "maybe it couldn't," but would be one
Who wouldn't say so till he'd tried.
So he buckled right in with the trace of a grin
On his face. If he worried he hid it.
He started to sing as he tackled the thing
That couldn't be done, and he did it.

Somebody scoffed: "Oh, you'll never do that;
At least no one ever has done it;"
But he took off his coat and he took off his hat,

And the first thing we knew he'd begun it.
With a lift of his chin and a bit of a grin,
Without any doubting or quiddit,
He started to sing as he tackled the thing
That couldn't be done, and he did it.

There are thousands to tell you it cannot be done,
There are thousands to prophesy failure;
There are thousands to point out to you, one by one,
The dangers that wait to assail you.
But just buckle in with a bit of a grin,
Just take off your coat and go to it;
Just start to sing as you tackle the thing
That "cannot be done," and you'll do it.
        — Edgar A. Guest

Today's Quote: *He who governed the world before I was born shall take care of it likewise when I am dead. My part is to improve the present moment.* — John Wesley

Today's Verse: Whoever would love life and see good days must keep his tongue from evil and his lips from deceitful speech. He must turn from evil and do good; he must seek peace and pursue it (1 Pet. 3:10-11).

What Is Really Important in Life?

GEORGE WASHINGTON CARVER was a man who lived with purpose, goodness, and balance. Born as a slave into a family of slaves, Carver struggled against tremendous odds to finally achieve a formal education. After years of abuse he did finish his master's degree and was invited to accept a position with Iowa University in Iowa City. It was a coveted position and no other black had ever been appointed to such a prestigious faculty in that university. Other members of the faculty and administration at the university learned to love him and students eagerly sought to be in his classes. Life was wonderful for Carver for the first time in his life.

Then . . . a letter arrived from Booker T. Washington asking the young scientist, Carver, to join together with him in a dream to educate the blacks of the South. After some soul-searching he resigned from the faculty of Iowa U. to give himself to the dream of Washington. Leaving the comforts of his prestigious position, Carver traveled to the parched cotton fields of the South to live and work and educate his starving people. People were not only starved for food but for learning and the opportunity to do better. Years of sacrifice and many insults followed . . . but surely and slowly this great soul began to make his mark. Education brought his people a dignity that would raise them forever from the slave class.

Whenever he was questioned about his committment and brilliance as a scientist, Carver always said that the good Lord gave him everything. One unheard of characteristic was that he refused to accept money for any of his discoveries and would freely give those secrets to anyone who asked for them or their use! Three presidents would claim him as their friend and confidant. Industries would vie for his services. Would you believe that Thomas Edison offered him a beautiful new laboratory to be built to his specifications along with an unheard of salary in his day, $100,000 per year, if he would bring his services to the Edison laboratories?

When Carver turned down this very lucrative and enticing offer, some of his critics commented and questioned his motives. He was challenged: "If you had all this money you could help your people."

Carver simply replied, "If I had all that money I might forget my people."

The epitaph on his tomb sums up his life: "He could have added fame and fortune, but cared for neither, he found happiness and honor in being helpful to the world."

Today's Quote: *Sacrifice is only that which is given after the heart has given all that it can spare.*

Today's Verse: Greater love has no one than this, that he lay down his life for his friends (John 15:13).

The Animal School

Once upon a time, the animals decided they must do something special to meet the problems of a "new world." So they organized a school.

They adopted an activity curriculum consisting of running, climbing, swimming, and flying. To make it easier to administer the curriculum, all the animals took all the subjects.

The duck was excellent in swimming, in fact better than his instructor, but he made only passing grades in flying and was very poor in running.

The rabbit started at the top of the class in running, but had a nervous breakdown because of so much make-up work in swimming.

The squirrel was excellent in climbing until he developed frustration in the flying class where his teacher made him start from the ground up instead of from the treetop down. He developed a "charlie horse" and then got a C in climbing and a D in running.

The eagle was a problem child and was disciplined severely. In the climbing class he beat all the others to the top of the tree, but insisted on using his own way to get there.

At the end of the year, an abnormal eel who could swim exceedingly well, and also run, climb, and fly a little, had the highest average and was valedictorian.

The prairie dogs stayed out of school and fought the tax levy because the administration would not add burrowing to the curriculum. They apprenticed their children to the badger and later joined the groundhogs and gophers to start a successful private school.[14]

Does this fable have a moral?

And does the moral have an application? Yes, lots of applications. Probably the most important is the process of attempting to fit every one into the same mold. The lives we are touching are impressionable, printable, moldable — but how are we pressing and forming and guiding? Do we insist that all must look alike when their education is completed? When they graduate are they still as excited about learning as when they began? God created each individual with uniqueness that is not shared by anyone else — different fingerprints, personal DNAs. There are no copies. Why is a bronze by Degas or a violin by Stradivarius or a painting by Rembrandt so valuable? They each had a unique creator and are so rare in number. Think a moment about what makes people so valuable — who created them?

Today's Quote: *The world and people God made were beautiful. The ugliness is mankind's own idea.*

Today's Verse: I will praise You, for I am fearfully and wonderfully made; Marvelous are Your works, And that my soul knows very well (Ps. 139:14;NKJV).

Who Did You Say?

A teacher of English Literature began her class session by challenging her students to identify this poem and the author:

Listen my children and you shall hear
Of the midnight ride of Paul Revere,
On the 18th of April in 75;
Hardly a man is now alive
Who remembers that famous day and year.

The first hand that went up got it right, "Teacher, that is the first verse of Henry Wadsworth Longfellow's poem, "Paul Revere's Ride." Then she read the last four lines of the poem, not quite as familiar as the first verse:

In the hour of darkness and peril and need,
The people will waken and listen to hear
The hurrying hoofbeats of that steed,
And the midnight message of Paul Revere.

The teacher's question this time was, "What was the name of Paul Revere's horse?" The students were then assigned to read all 13 verses to see if anyone could come up with the name of his trusty horse. The horse is mentioned a number of times but the name is never given.

What's the point this teacher was attempting to get across? That while Paul Revere got all the mention and glory, some unknown horse made a most significant contribution in order to make the famous ride possible. Now I'm also aware that many historians feel that this poem gives Revere more credit than should have been due to him, but that's another issue.

While Emmit Smith of the Dallas Cowboys gets the credit for another record-setting year of carrying the football, very few can name the players in front of him who do the blocking to open up the holes through which he makes his spectacular runs.

No one who experiences any kind of success in life does it completely alone. We have all received support from some behind-the-scenes person, be it a friend, parents, teacher, or mentor. Let's learn to share the credit where credit is also due.

Today's Quote: *The be-all and end-all of life should not be to get rich, but to enrich the world.* — B. C. Forbes

Today's Verse: Tychicus, the dear brother and faithful servant in the Lord, will tell you everything, so that you also may know how I am and what I am doing. I am sending him to you for this very purpose (Eph. 6:21-22).

NOTES

1. AP, *News Leader*, Springfield, Missouri, 3/19/94.

2. Robert Fulghum, *All I Really Need to Know I Learned in Kindergarten* (New York, NY: Ivy Books, 1989), page 4-5.

3. Jack Canfield and Mark Hansen, quoting Art Buchwald, *Chicken Soup for the Soul* (Deerfield Beach, FL: Health Communications), page 32-34.

4. John Schlatter, motivational speaker, Cypress, CA.

5. Brian Cavanaugh, *More Sower's Seeds* (Mahway, NJ: Paulist Press, 1992), page 31-32.

6. Mildred Lewis, motivational speaker, Berryville, AR.

7. Camille Shirah, *Teachers in Focus,* January 1995, page 13.

8. Kelli Anderson, *Sports Illustrated* 2/21/93.

9. Jack Canfield and Mark Hansen, *A 2nd Helping of Chicken Soup for the Soul* (Deerfield Beach, FL: Health Communications, Inc., 1995).

10. Eric W. Johnson, *Humorous Stories about the Human Condition* (Del Mar, CA: Prometheus Books).

11. Norman Vincent Peale, *Treasury of Joy and Enthusiasm* (Old Tappan, NJ: Fleming H. Revell, 1981), page 61.

12. Author unknown.

13. Gary Smalley and John Trent, *The Blessing* (Colorado Springs, CO: NavPress, 1988).

14. George H. Reavis.